Wellness Journal

Printed in the USA by A2Z Books, LLC. Copyright by Dr. Synovia Dover-Harris of A2Z Books Publishing. All rights reserved. This book or any portion thereof may not be reproduced or used in any manner whatsoever without the express written permission of the publisher except for the use of brief quotations in book review Printed in the United Stated. First Printing
ISBN 978-1-943284-69-6
www.A2ZBookspublishing.net

Welcome to the Ultimate Wellness Journal

Hi I'm Dr. Synovia CEO of A2Z Books Publishing. I started my wellness journey over a decade ago, because at the time I was working on my doctorate degree, I was teaching college, I was launching my publishing company, I was married with 2 little girls and I had other businesses that took up all of my time and energy. I was sitting on 2 boards and had lots of toxic friendships. I knew that I wanted to experience a better, more fulfilling life, so I decided to start my wellness journey in the hopes to find the highest level of bliss. I started working out daily, eating right, getting rid of bad relationships and I started journaling. It was not an easy transition, however throughout the years I have been able to reach what I see as my level of wellness and happiness in my life. I had students and clients ask me how do I hold it all together and be soooo happy doing it. So I decided to start jotting some of the things down that I did and decided to create this Well Wellness Journal to help you live your best life.

Dr. Synovia
CEO of A2Z Books Publishing

This Wellness Journal Belongs to:

Wellness is the compete integration of body, mind, and spirit – the realization that everything we do, think, feel, and believe has an effect on our state of well-being.
Greg Anderson

Google defines Wellness as

well•ness

/ˈwelnəs/

noun

the state of being in good health, especially as an actively pursued goal.

Wellness is also defined as:

Being healthy and happy simultaneously and maintaining that state.

I am going to Define Wellness as (Define wellness for yourself here).

He who takes medicine and neglects to diet wastes the skill of his doctors.
Chinese Proverbs

Wellness
Quarter 1

Am I Living in a *State of Wellness?*

☐ Yes ☐ No

If I answered yes, how do I know I am living in a state of Wellness?

If I answered no, what changes do I need to make to be living in a state of Wellness?

Am I in a *good mood?*

Yes   No

If I answered yes, how do I know I am in a good mood?

If I answered no, what changes do I need to make in my life to be in good mood?

Am I healthy *(mentally and physically)*?

☐ Yes   ☐ No

If I answered yes, what am I doing to remain healthy mentally and physically?

If I answered no, what changes do I need to make to become healthy mentally and physically?

Wellness Prompt #1

Write 5 things that make you happy:

1.

2.

3.

4.

5.

Wellness Prompt #2

Write 5 things you like to do:

1.

2.

3.

4.

5.

Wellness Prompt #3

Write 5 Things You Love About Your Life:

1.

2.

3.

4.

5.

Wellness Prompt #4

Write 5 Things You Live By:

1.

2.

3.

4.

5.

Wellness Prompt #5

Write 5 Things You Want in Life:

1.

2.

3.

4.

5.

Wellness Calendar

(Use this calendar to track your wellness journey) You can add Doctor's appointments, dinner dates, a nap and everything else that will help you to remain well.

SUN	MON	TUE	WED	THU	FRI	SAT

Weekly Wellness Tracker

Am I Exercising?   Yes   No

What exercise have I done?

Am I eating right?   Yes   No

What am I eating?

Am I drinking water?   Yes   No

How much water am I drinking?

Am I taking my vitamins?   Yes   No

What vitamins am I taking?

Am I getting adequate Sleep?   Yes   No

How much sleep am I getting?

Journal Here

(Journaling is a practice used to ease the mind, reduce stress and anxiety.) Write What's on Your Mind.

_____
_____
_____
_____
_____
_____
_____
_____
_____
_____
_____
_____
_____

Weekly Wellness Tracker

Am I Exercising?   Yes   No

What exercise have I done?

Am I eating right?   Yes   No

What am I eating?

Am I drinking water?   Yes   No

How much water am I drinking?

Am I taking my vitamins?   Yes   No

What vitamins am I taking?

Am I getting adequate Sleep?   Yes   No

How much sleep am I getting?

Journal Here

(Journaling is a practice used to ease the mind, reduce stress and anxiety.) Write What's on Your Mind.

Weekly Wellness Tracker

Am I Exercising?   Yes   No

What exercise have I done?

Am I eating right?   Yes   No

What am I eating?

Am I drinking water?   Yes   No

How much water am I drinking?

Am I taking my vitamins?   Yes   No

What vitamins am I taking?

Am I getting adequate Sleep?   Yes   No

How much sleep am I getting?

Journal Here

(Journaling is a practice used to ease the mind, reduce stress and anxiety.) Write What's on Your Mind.

Weekly Wellness Tracker

Am I Exercising?   Yes   No

What exercise have I done?

Am I eating right?   Yes   No

What am I eating?

Am I drinking water?   Yes   No

How much water am I drinking?

Am I taking my vitamins?   Yes   No

What vitamins am I taking?

Am I getting adequate Sleep?   Yes   No

How much sleep am I getting?

WELLNESS AFFIRMATION
Today I am Healthy

Wellness Calendar

(Use this calendar to track your wellness journey) You can add Doctor's appointments, dinner dates, a nap and everything else that will help you to remain well.

SUN	MON	TUE	WED	THU	FRI	SAT

Weekly Wellness Tracker

Am I Exercising?   Yes   No

What exercise have I done?

Am I eating right?   Yes   No

What am I eating?

Am I drinking water?   Yes   No

How much water am I drinking?

Am I taking my vitamins?   Yes   No

What vitamins am I taking?

Am I getting adequate Sleep?   Yes   No

How much sleep am I getting?

Journal Here

(Journaling is a practice used to ease the mind, reduce stress and anxiety.) Write What's on Your Mind.

_____
_____
_____
_____
_____
_____
_____
_____
_____
_____
_____
_____
_____
_____

Weekly Wellness Tracker

Am I Exercising?   Yes   No

What exercise have I done?

Am I eating right?   Yes   No

What am I eating?

Am I drinking water?   Yes   No

How much water am I drinking?

Am I taking my vitamins?   Yes   No

What vitamins am I taking?

Am I getting adequate Sleep?   Yes   No

How much sleep am I getting?

Journal Here

(Journaling is a practice used to ease the mind, reduce stress and anxiety.) Write What's on Your Mind.

_____

_____

_____

_____

_____

_____

_____

_____

_____

_____

_____

_____

_____

_____

Weekly Wellness Tracker

Am I Exercising?   Yes   No

What exercise have I done?

Am I eating right?   Yes   No

What am I eating?

Am I drinking water?   Yes   No

How much water am I drinking?

Am I taking my vitamins?   Yes   No

What vitamins am I taking?

Am I getting adequate Sleep?   Yes   No

How much sleep am I getting?

Journal Here

(Journaling is a practice used to ease the mind, reduce stress and anxiety.) Write What's on Your Mind.

_____
_____
_____
_____
_____
_____
_____
_____
_____
_____
_____
_____
_____
_____
_____
_____

Weekly Wellness Tracker

Am I Exercising? Yes No

What exercise have I done?

Am I eating right? Yes No

What am I eating?

Am I drinking water? Yes No

How much water am I drinking?

Am I taking my vitamins? Yes No

What vitamins am I taking?

Am I getting adequate Sleep? Yes No

How much sleep am I getting?

WELLNESS AFFIRMATION
Today I Well

Wellness Calendar

(Use this calendar to track your wellness journey) You can add Doctor's appointments, dinner dates, a nap and everything else that will help you to remain well.

SUN	MON	TUE	WED	THU	FRI	SAT

Weekly Wellness Tracker

Am I Exercising?   Yes   No

What exercise have I done?

Am I eating right?   Yes   No

What am I eating?

Am I drinking water?   Yes   No

How much water am I drinking?

Am I taking my vitamins?   Yes   No

What vitamins am I taking?

Am I getting adequate Sleep?   Yes   No

How much sleep am I getting?

Journal Here

(Journaling is a practice used to ease the mind, reduce stress and anxiety.) Write What's on Your Mind.

Weekly Wellness Tracker

Am I Exercising?   Yes   No

What exercise have I done?

Am I eating right?   Yes   No

What am I eating?

Am I drinking water?   Yes   No

How much water am I drinking?

Am I taking my vitamins?   Yes   No

What vitamins am I taking?

Am I getting adequate Sleep?   Yes   No

How much sleep am I getting?

Journal Here

(Journaling is a practice used to ease the mind, reduce stress and anxiety.) Write What's on Your Mind.

_____
_____
_____
_____
_____
_____
_____
_____
_____
_____
_____
_____
_____
_____

Weekly Wellness Tracker

Am I Exercising?   Yes   No

What exercise have I done?

_____

_____

Am I eating right?   Yes   No

What am I eating?

_____

_____

Am I drinking water?   Yes   No

How much water am I drinking?

_____

_____

Am I taking my vitamins?   Yes   No

What vitamins am I taking?

_____

_____

Am I getting adequate Sleep?   Yes   No

How much sleep am I getting?

_____

Journal Here

(Journaling is a practice used to ease the mind, reduce stress and anxiety.) Write What's on Your Mind.

Weekly Wellness Tracker

Am I Exercising?   Yes   No

What exercise have I done?

Am I eating right?   Yes   No

What am I eating?

Am I drinking water?   Yes   No

How much water am I drinking?

Am I taking my vitamins?   Yes   No

What vitamins am I taking?

Am I getting adequate Sleep?   Yes   No

How much sleep am I getting?

WELLNESS AFFIRMATION
Today I am Restored

The trouble with always trying to preserve the health of the body is that it is so difficult to do without destroying the health of the mind.
G.K. Chesterton

Am I Living in a *State of Wellness?*

Yes   No

If I answered yes, how do I know I am living in a state of Wellness?

If I answered no, what changes do I need to make to be living in a state of Wellness?

Am I in a *good mood?*

Yes   No

If I answered yes, how do I know I am in a good mood?

If I answered no, what changes do I need to make in my life to be in good mood?

Am I healthy *(mentally and physically)*?

◯ Yes   ◯ No

If I answered yes, what am I doing to remain healthy mentally and physically?

If I answered no, what changes do I need to make to become healthy mentally and physically?

Wellness Prompt #1

Write 5 things that make you happy:

1.

2.

3.

4.

5.

Wellness Prompt #2

Write 5 things you like to do:

1.

2.

3.

4.

5.

Wellness Prompt #3

Write 5 Things You Love About Your Life:

1.

2.

3.

4.

5.

Wellness Prompt #4

Write 5 Things You Live By:

1.

2.

3.

4.

5.

Wellness Prompt #5

Write 5 Things You Want in Life:

1.

2.

3.

4.

5.

Wellness Calendar

(Use this calendar to track your wellness journey) You can add Doctor's appointments, dinner dates, a nap and everything else that will help you to remain well.

SUN	MON	TUE	WED	THU	FRI	SAT

Weekly Wellness Tracker

Am I Exercising?   Yes   No

What exercise have I done?

Am I eating right?   Yes   No

What am I eating?

Am I drinking water?   Yes   No

How much water am I drinking?

Am I taking my vitamins?   Yes   No

What vitamins am I taking?

Am I getting adequate Sleep?   Yes   No

How much sleep am I getting?

Journal Here

(Journaling is a practice used to ease the mind, reduce stress and anxiety.) Write What's on Your Mind.

Weekly Wellness Tracker

Am I Exercising?   Yes   No

What exercise have I done?

Am I eating right?   Yes   No

What am I eating?

Am I drinking water?   Yes   No

How much water am I drinking?

Am I taking my vitamins?   Yes   No

What vitamins am I taking?

Am I getting adequate Sleep?   Yes   No

How much sleep am I getting?

Journal Here

(Journaling is a practice used to ease the mind, reduce stress and anxiety.) Write What's on Your Mind.

Weekly Wellness Tracker

Am I Exercising?   Yes   No

What exercise have I done?

Am I eating right?   Yes   No

What am I eating?

Am I drinking water?   Yes   No

How much water am I drinking?

Am I taking my vitamins?   Yes   No

What vitamins am I taking?

Am I getting adequate Sleep?   Yes   No

How much sleep am I getting?

Journal Here

(Journaling is a practice used to ease the mind, reduce stress and anxiety.) Write What's on Your Mind.

Weekly Wellness Tracker

Am I Exercising?   Yes   No

What exercise have I done?

Am I eating right?   Yes   No

What am I eating?

Am I drinking water?   Yes   No

How much water am I drinking?

Am I taking my vitamins?   Yes   No

What vitamins am I taking?

Am I getting adequate Sleep?   Yes   No

How much sleep am I getting?

WELLNESS AFFIRMATION
Today I Well

Wellness Calendar

(Use this calendar to track your wellness journey) You can add Doctor's appointments, dinner dates, a nap and everything else that will help you to remain well.

SUN	MON	TUE	WED	THU	FRI	SAT

Weekly Wellness Tracker

Am I Exercising?   Yes   No

What exercise have I done?

Am I eating right?   Yes   No

What am I eating?

Am I drinking water?   Yes   No

How much water am I drinking?

Am I taking my vitamins?   Yes   No

What vitamins am I taking?

Am I getting adequate Sleep?   Yes   No

How much sleep am I getting?

Journal Here

(Journaling is a practice used to ease the mind, reduce stress and anxiety.) Write What's on Your Mind.

Weekly Wellness Tracker

Am I Exercising?   Yes   No

What exercise have I done?

Am I eating right?   Yes   No

What am I eating?

Am I drinking water?   Yes   No

How much water am I drinking?

Am I taking my vitamins?   Yes   No

What vitamins am I taking?

Am I getting adequate Sleep?   Yes   No

How much sleep am I getting?

Journal Here

(Journaling is a practice used to ease the mind, reduce stress and anxiety.) Write What's on Your Mind.

_____
_____
_____
_____
_____
_____
_____
_____
_____
_____
_____
_____
_____
_____
_____

Weekly Wellness Tracker

Am I Exercising?   Yes   No

What exercise have I done?

Am I eating right?   Yes   No

What am I eating?

Am I drinking water?   Yes   No

How much water am I drinking?

Am I taking my vitamins?   Yes   No

What vitamins am I taking?

Am I getting adequate Sleep?   Yes   No

How much sleep am I getting?

Journal Here

(Journaling is a practice used to ease the mind, reduce stress and anxiety.) Write What's on Your Mind.

Weekly Wellness Tracker

Am I Exercising? Yes No

What exercise have I done?

Am I eating right? Yes No

What am I eating?

Am I drinking water? Yes No

How much water am I drinking?

Am I taking my vitamins? Yes No

What vitamins am I taking?

Am I getting adequate Sleep? Yes No

How much sleep am I getting?

WELLNESS AFFIRMATION
Today I am Loved

Wellness Calendar

(Use this calendar to track your wellness journey) You can add Doctor's appointments, dinner dates, a nap and everything else that will help you to remain well.

SUN	MON	TUE	WED	THU	FRI	SAT

Weekly Wellness Tracker

Am I Exercising?   Yes   No

What exercise have I done?

Am I eating right?   Yes   No

What am I eating?

Am I drinking water?   Yes   No

How much water am I drinking?

Am I taking my vitamins?   Yes   No

What vitamins am I taking?

Am I getting adequate Sleep?   Yes   No

How much sleep am I getting?

Journal Here

(Journaling is a practice used to ease the mind, reduce stress and anxiety.) Write What's on Your Mind.

_____
_____
_____
_____
_____
_____
_____
_____
_____
_____
_____
_____
_____
_____

Weekly Wellness Tracker

Am I Exercising?   Yes   No

What exercise have I done?

Am I eating right?   Yes   No

What am I eating?

Am I drinking water?   Yes   No

How much water am I drinking?

Am I taking my vitamins?   Yes   No

What vitamins am I taking?

Am I getting adequate Sleep?   Yes   No

How much sleep am I getting?

Journal Here

(Journaling is a practice used to ease the mind, reduce stress and anxiety.) Write What's on Your Mind.

Weekly Wellness Tracker

Am I Exercising?   Yes   No

What exercise have I done?

Am I eating right?   Yes   No

What am I eating?

Am I drinking water?   Yes   No

How much water am I drinking?

Am I taking my vitamins?   Yes   No

What vitamins am I taking?

Am I getting adequate Sleep?   Yes   No

How much sleep am I getting?

Journal Here

(Journaling is a practice used to ease the mind, reduce stress and anxiety.) Write What's on Your Mind.

_____
_____
_____
_____
_____
_____
_____
_____
_____
_____
_____
_____
_____
_____

Weekly Wellness Tracker

Am I Exercising?   Yes   No

What exercise have I done?

Am I eating right?   Yes   No

What am I eating?

Am I drinking water?   Yes   No

How much water am I drinking?

Am I taking my vitamins?   Yes   No

What vitamins am I taking?

Am I getting adequate Sleep?   Yes   No

How much sleep am I getting?

WELLNESS AFFIRMATION
Today I am at Peace

So many people spend their health gaining wealth, and then have to spend their wealth to regain their health.
A.J. Reb Materi

Wellness
Quarter 3

Am I Living in a *State of Wellness?*

Yes   No

If I answered yes, how do I know I am living in a state of Wellness?

If I answered no, what changes do I need to make to be living in a state of Wellness?

Am I in a *good mood?*

Yes   No

If I answered yes, how do I know I am in a good mood?

If I answered no, what changes do I need to make in my life to be in good mood?

Am I healthy *(mentally and physically)?*

☐ Yes ☐ No

If I answered yes, what am I doing to remain healthy mentally and physically?

If I answered no, what changes do I need to make to become healthy mentally and physically?

Wellness Prompt #1

Write 5 things that make you happy:

1.

2.

3.

4.

5.

Wellness Prompt #2

Write 5 things you like to do:

1.

2.

3.

4.

5.

Wellness Prompt #3

Write 5 Things You Love About Your Life:

1.

2.

3.

4.

5.

Wellness Prompt #4

Write 5 Things You Live By:

1.

2.

3.

4.

5.

Wellness Prompt #5

Write 5 Things You Want in Life:

1.

2.

3.

4.

5.

Wellness Calendar

(Use this calendar to track your wellness journey) You can add Doctor's appointments, dinner dates, a nap and everything else that will help you to remain well.

SUN	MON	TUE	WED	THU	FRI	SAT

Weekly Wellness Tracker

Am I Exercising?   Yes   No

What exercise have I done?

Am I eating right?   Yes   No

What am I eating?

Am I drinking water?   Yes   No

How much water am I drinking?

Am I taking my vitamins?   Yes   No

What vitamins am I taking?

Am I getting adequate Sleep?   Yes   No

How much sleep am I getting?

Journal Here

(Journaling is a practice used to ease the mind, reduce stress and anxiety.) Write What's on Your Mind.

Weekly Wellness Tracker

Am I Exercising?   Yes   No

What exercise have I done?

Am I eating right?   Yes   No

What am I eating?

Am I drinking water?   Yes   No

How much water am I drinking?

Am I taking my vitamins?   Yes   No

What vitamins am I taking?

Am I getting adequate Sleep?   Yes   No

How much sleep am I getting?

Journal Here

(Journaling is a practice used to ease the mind, reduce stress and anxiety.) Write What's on Your Mind.

_____

_____

_____

_____

_____

_____

_____

_____

_____

_____

_____

_____

_____

_____

Weekly Wellness Tracker

Am I Exercising?   Yes   No

What exercise have I done?

Am I eating right?   Yes   No

What am I eating?

Am I drinking water?   Yes   No

How much water am I drinking?

Am I taking my vitamins?   Yes   No

What vitamins am I taking?

Am I getting adequate Sleep?   Yes   No

How much sleep am I getting?

Journal Here

(Journaling is a practice used to ease the mind, reduce stress and anxiety.) Write What's on Your Mind.

_____
_____
_____
_____
_____
_____
_____
_____
_____
_____
_____
_____
_____
_____

Weekly Wellness Tracker

Am I Exercising?   Yes   No

What exercise have I done?

Am I eating right?   Yes   No

What am I eating?

Am I drinking water?   Yes   No

How much water am I drinking?

Am I taking my vitamins?   Yes   No

What vitamins am I taking?

Am I getting adequate Sleep?   Yes   No

How much sleep am I getting?

WELLNESS AFFIRMATION
Today I am Happy

Wellness Calendar

(Use this calendar to track your wellness journey) You can add Doctor's appointments, dinner dates, a nap and everything else that will help you to remain well.

SUN	MON	TUE	WED	THU	FRI	SAT

Weekly Wellness Tracker

Am I Exercising?   Yes   No

What exercise have I done?

Am I eating right?   Yes   No

What am I eating?

Am I drinking water?   Yes   No

How much water am I drinking?

Am I taking my vitamins?   Yes   No

What vitamins am I taking?

Am I getting adequate Sleep?   Yes   No

How much sleep am I getting?

Journal Here

(Journaling is a practice used to ease the mind, reduce stress and anxiety.) Write What's on Your Mind.

_____
_____
_____
_____
_____
_____
_____
_____
_____
_____
_____
_____
_____
_____

Weekly Wellness Tracker

Am I Exercising?   Yes   No

What exercise have I done?

Am I eating right?   Yes   No

What am I eating?

Am I drinking water?   Yes   No

How much water am I drinking?

Am I taking my vitamins?   Yes   No

What vitamins am I taking?

Am I getting adequate Sleep?   Yes   No

How much sleep am I getting?

Journal Here

(Journaling is a practice used to ease the mind, reduce stress and anxiety.) Write What's on Your Mind.

_____
_____
_____
_____
_____
_____
_____
_____
_____
_____
_____
_____
_____
_____
_____
_____

Weekly Wellness Tracker

Am I Exercising?   Yes   No

What exercise have I done?

Am I eating right?   Yes   No

What am I eating?

Am I drinking water?   Yes   No

How much water am I drinking?

Am I taking my vitamins?   Yes   No

What vitamins am I taking?

Am I getting adequate Sleep?   Yes   No

How much sleep am I getting?

Journal Here

(Journaling is a practice used to ease the mind, reduce stress and anxiety.) Write What's on Your Mind.

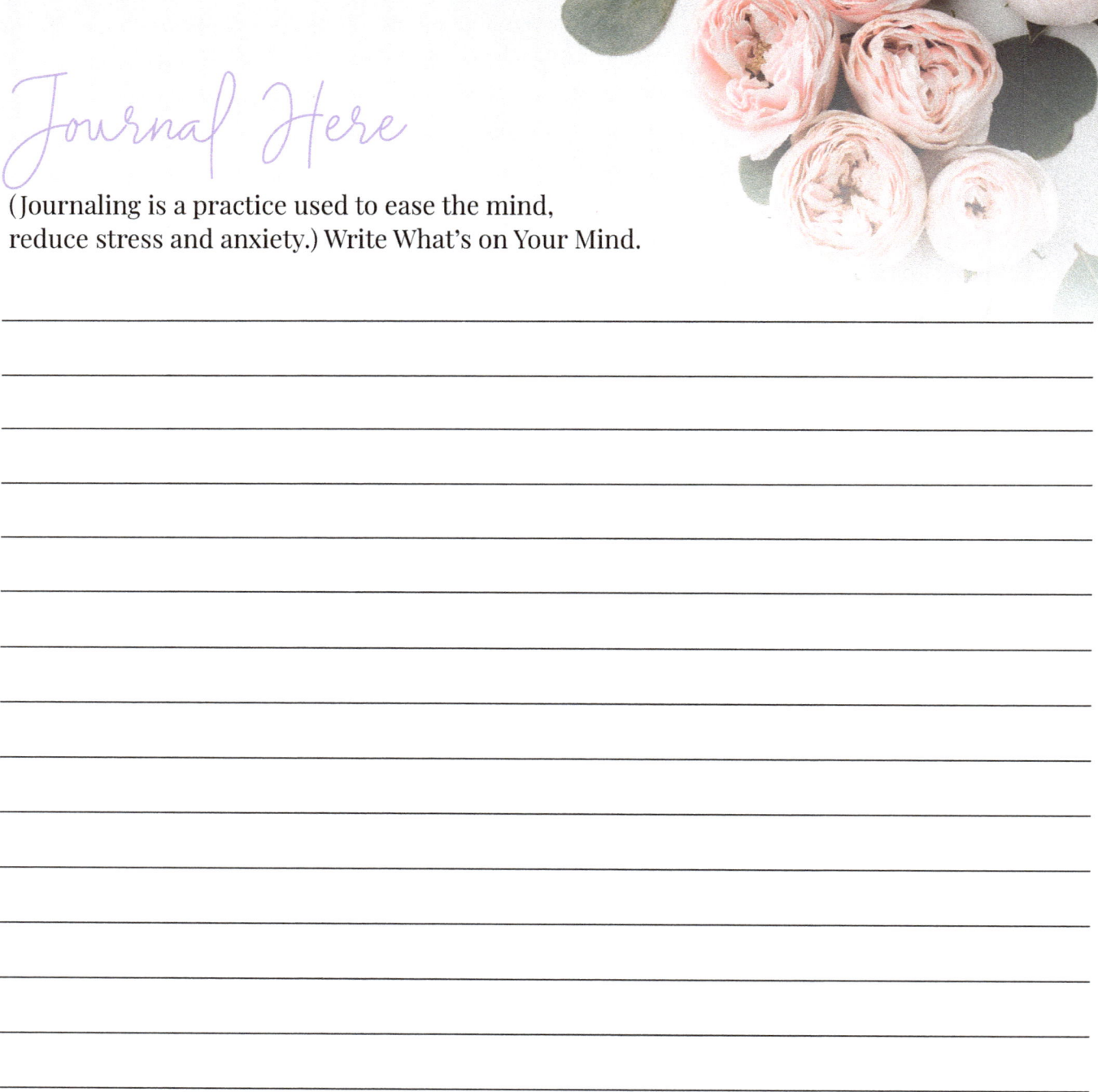

Weekly Wellness Tracker

Am I Exercising?   Yes   No

What exercise have I done?

Am I eating right?   Yes   No

What am I eating?

Am I drinking water?   Yes   No

How much water am I drinking?

Am I taking my vitamins?   Yes   No

What vitamins am I taking?

Am I getting adequate Sleep?   Yes   No

How much sleep am I getting?

WELLNESS AFFIRMATION
Today I am Healthy

Wellness Calendar

(Use this calendar to track your wellness journey) You can add Doctor's appointments, dinner dates, a nap and everything else that will help you to remain well.

SUN	MON	TUE	WED	THU	FRI	SAT

Weekly Wellness Tracker

Am I Exercising?   Yes   No
What exercise have I done?

Am I eating right?   Yes   No
What am I eating?

Am I drinking water?   Yes   No
How much water am I drinking?

Am I taking my vitamins?   Yes   No
What vitamins am I taking?

Am I getting adequate Sleep?   Yes   No
How much sleep am I getting?

Journal Here

(Journaling is a practice used to ease the mind, reduce stress and anxiety.) Write What's on Your Mind.

Weekly Wellness Tracker

Am I Exercising?	Yes	No

What exercise have I done?

Am I eating right?	Yes	No

What am I eating?

Am I drinking water?	Yes	No

How much water am I drinking?

Am I taking my vitamins?	Yes	No

What vitamins am I taking?

Am I getting adequate Sleep?	Yes	No

How much sleep am I getting?

Journal Here

(Journaling is a practice used to ease the mind, reduce stress and anxiety.) Write What's on Your Mind.

Weekly Wellness Tracker

Am I Exercising?   Yes   No

What exercise have I done?

Am I eating right?   Yes   No

What am I eating?

Am I drinking water?   Yes   No

How much water am I drinking?

Am I taking my vitamins?   Yes   No

What vitamins am I taking?

Am I getting adequate Sleep?   Yes   No

How much sleep am I getting?

Journal Here

(Journaling is a practice used to ease the mind, reduce stress and anxiety.) Write What's on Your Mind.

Weekly Wellness Tracker

Am I Exercising?   Yes   No

What exercise have I done?

Am I eating right?   Yes   No

What am I eating?

Am I drinking water?   Yes   No

How much water am I drinking?

Am I taking my vitamins?   Yes   No

What vitamins am I taking?

Am I getting adequate Sleep?   Yes   No

How much sleep am I getting?

Health is a state of complete harmony of the body, mind and spirit. When one is free from physical disabilities and mental distractions, the gates of the soul open.
B.K.S. Iyengar

Wellness
Quarter 4

Am I Living in a *State of Wellness?*

Yes   No

If I answered yes, how do I know I am living in a state of Wellness?

If I answered no, what changes do I need to make to be living in a state of Wellness?

Am I in a *good mood?*

Yes	No

If I answered yes, how do I know I am in a good mood?

If I answered no, what changes do I need to make in my life to be in good mood?

Am I healthy *(mentally and physically)?*

Yes   No

If I answered yes, what am I doing to remain healthy mentally and physically?

If I answered no, what changes do I need to make to become healthy mentally and physically?

Wellness Prompt #1

Write 5 things that make you happy:

1.

2.

3.

4.

5.

Wellness Prompt #2

Write 5 things you like to do:

1.

2.

3.

4.

5.

Wellness Prompt #3

Write 5 Things You Love About Your Life:

1.

2.

3.

4.

5.

Wellness Prompt #4

Write 5 Things You Live By:

1.

2.

3.

4.

5.

Wellness Prompt #5

Write 5 Things You Want in Life:

1.

2.

3.

4.

5.

Wellness Calendar

(Use this calendar to track your wellness journey) You can add Doctor's appointments, dinner dates, a nap and everything else that will help you to remain well.

SUN	MON	TUE	WED	THU	FRI	SAT

Weekly Wellness Tracker

Am I Exercising?   Yes   No

What exercise have I done?

Am I eating right?   Yes   No

What am I eating?

Am I drinking water?   Yes   No

How much water am I drinking?

Am I taking my vitamins?   Yes   No

What vitamins am I taking?

Am I getting adequate Sleep?   Yes   No

How much sleep am I getting?

Journal Here

(Journaling is a practice used to ease the mind, reduce stress and anxiety.) Write What's on Your Mind.

_____
_____
_____
_____
_____
_____
_____
_____
_____
_____
_____
_____
_____
_____
_____

Weekly Wellness Tracker

Am I Exercising?   Yes   No

What exercise have I done?

Am I eating right?   Yes   No

What am I eating?

Am I drinking water?   Yes   No

How much water am I drinking?

Am I taking my vitamins?   Yes   No

What vitamins am I taking?

Am I getting adequate Sleep?   Yes   No

How much sleep am I getting?

Journal Here

(Journaling is a practice used to ease the mind, reduce stress and anxiety.) Write What's on Your Mind.

_____
_____
_____
_____
_____
_____
_____
_____
_____
_____
_____
_____
_____
_____
_____

Weekly Wellness Tracker

Am I Exercising?   Yes   No

What exercise have I done?

Am I eating right?   Yes   No

What am I eating?

Am I drinking water?   Yes   No

How much water am I drinking?

Am I taking my vitamins?   Yes   No

What vitamins am I taking?

Am I getting adequate Sleep?   Yes   No

How much sleep am I getting?

Journal Here

(Journaling is a practice used to ease the mind, reduce stress and anxiety.) Write What's on Your Mind.

_____
_____
_____
_____
_____
_____
_____
_____
_____
_____
_____
_____
_____
_____

Weekly Wellness Tracker

Am I Exercising?   Yes   No

What exercise have I done?

Am I eating right?   Yes   No

What am I eating?

Am I drinking water?   Yes   No

How much water am I drinking?

Am I taking my vitamins?   Yes   No

What vitamins am I taking?

Am I getting adequate Sleep?   Yes   No

How much sleep am I getting?

WELLNESS AFFIRMATION
Today I am Restored

Wellness Calendar

(Use this calendar to track your wellness journey) You can add Doctor's appointments, dinner dates, a nap and everything else that will help you to remain well.

SUN	MON	TUE	WED	THU	FRI	SAT

Weekly Wellness Tracker

Am I Exercising?   Yes   No

What exercise have I done?

Am I eating right?   Yes   No

What am I eating?

Am I drinking water?   Yes   No

How much water am I drinking?

Am I taking my vitamins?   Yes   No

What vitamins am I taking?

Am I getting adequate Sleep?   Yes   No

How much sleep am I getting?

Journal Here

(Journaling is a practice used to ease the mind, reduce stress and anxiety.) Write What's on Your Mind.

Weekly Wellness Tracker

Am I Exercising?   Yes   No

What exercise have I done?

Am I eating right?   Yes   No

What am I eating?

Am I drinking water?   Yes   No

How much water am I drinking?

Am I taking my vitamins?   Yes   No

What vitamins am I taking?

Am I getting adequate Sleep?   Yes   No

How much sleep am I getting?

Journal Here

(Journaling is a practice used to ease the mind, reduce stress and anxiety.) Write What's on Your Mind.

Weekly Wellness Tracker

Am I Exercising?   Yes   No

What exercise have I done?

Am I eating right?   Yes   No

What am I eating?

Am I drinking water?   Yes   No

How much water am I drinking?

Am I taking my vitamins?   Yes   No

What vitamins am I taking?

Am I getting adequate Sleep?   Yes   No

How much sleep am I getting?

Journal Here

(Journaling is a practice used to ease the mind, reduce stress and anxiety.) Write What's on Your Mind.

_____

_____

_____

_____

_____

_____

_____

_____

_____

_____

_____

_____

_____

Weekly Wellness Tracker

Am I Exercising?   Yes   No

What exercise have I done?

Am I eating right?   Yes   No

What am I eating?

Am I drinking water?   Yes   No

How much water am I drinking?

Am I taking my vitamins?   Yes   No

What vitamins am I taking?

Am I getting adequate Sleep?   Yes   No

How much sleep am I getting?

WELLNESS AFFIRMATION
Today I am Loved

Wellness Calendar

(Use this calendar to track your wellness journey) You can add Doctor's appointments, dinner dates, a nap and everything else that will help you to remain well.

SUN	MON	TUE	WED	THU	FRI	SAT

Weekly Wellness Tracker

Am I Exercising?   Yes   No

What exercise have I done?

Am I eating right?   Yes   No

What am I eating?

Am I drinking water?   Yes   No

How much water am I drinking?

Am I taking my vitamins?   Yes   No

What vitamins am I taking?

Am I getting adequate Sleep?   Yes   No

How much sleep am I getting?

Journal Here

(Journaling is a practice used to ease the mind, reduce stress and anxiety.) Write What's on Your Mind.

_____
_____
_____
_____
_____
_____
_____
_____
_____
_____
_____
_____
_____
_____
_____

Weekly Wellness Tracker

Am I Exercising?   Yes   No

What exercise have I done?

Am I eating right?   Yes   No

What am I eating?

Am I drinking water?   Yes   No

How much water am I drinking?

Am I taking my vitamins?   Yes   No

What vitamins am I taking?

Am I getting adequate Sleep?   Yes   No

How much sleep am I getting?

Journal Here

(Journaling is a practice used to ease the mind, reduce stress and anxiety.) Write What's on Your Mind.

_____
_____
_____
_____
_____
_____
_____
_____
_____
_____
_____
_____
_____
_____
_____

Weekly Wellness Tracker

Am I Exercising?   Yes   No

What exercise have I done?

Am I eating right?   Yes   No

What am I eating?

Am I drinking water?   Yes   No

How much water am I drinking?

Am I taking my vitamins?   Yes   No

What vitamins am I taking?

Am I getting adequate Sleep?   Yes   No

How much sleep am I getting?

Journal Here

(Journaling is a practice used to ease the mind, reduce stress and anxiety.) Write What's on Your Mind.

Weekly Wellness Tracker

Am I Exercising?   Yes   No

What exercise have I done?

Am I eating right?   Yes   No

What am I eating?

Am I drinking water?   Yes   No

How much water am I drinking?

Am I taking my vitamins?   Yes   No

What vitamins am I taking?

Am I getting adequate Sleep?   Yes   No

How much sleep am I getting?

WELLNESS AFFIRMATION
Today I am at Peace

Interested In Writing/Publishing a book?
Contact @Dr.Synovia www.a2zbookspublishing.net

www.ingramcontent.com/pod-product-compliance
Lightning Source LLC
Chambersburg PA
CBHW051354110526
44592CB00024B/2978